CAMBRIDGE COLLEGE

by Janet Jeacock
East Anglia Registered Guide,
Cambridge Registered Guide,
Guild of Registered Tourist Guides

Cambridge, a name familiar the world over, is a many-faceted place that means different things to different people. To most of those who live there it is a proud, ancient and thriving market town, cooled by harsh winds from the uncompromising fens to the north; for others it is a new centre of commerce, warmed by international recognition of its success in marketing its technological innovation and enterprise; to millions around the globe Cambridge is Christmas Eve and the service of Nine Lessons and Carols, transmitted by television and radio from King's College Chapel.

Essentially, Cambridge owes its fame to the university which takes its name – a university with an enviable reputation for intellectual achievement and for the historical and architectural magnificence of its colleges. It is to those colleges that this book is devoted.

To begin, a brief look at the historical context. There has been human activity in the area since neolithic times, but it was with the arrival of the Romans that Cambridge began to assume importance. Their legions forded what we now know as the River Cam and made it an important link in their road, the Via Devana, between their headquarters garrison in Colchester and Lincoln. They built a fortified camp on Castle Hill, north of the river, and their settlement became a staging-post for the legions moving to northern campaigns.

When the Romans left Cambridge around AD 400, it was a busy and prosperous town, but Europe was sliding towards the Dark Ages and when, in 695, a group of monks came to Cambridge from Ely in search of a stone coffin in which to bury St Etheldreda, foundress of their monastery, they entered a settlement which was empty and devastated.

By the time the 'Domesday

The Senate House

Book' was compiled in 1085, the community had re-established itself with 2,000 inhabitants. The Normans recognised its importance, built a castle on the site of the Roman settlement and sought to contain the Saxon rebels entrenched in the sulphurous and dangerous fens.

Edward I (1239-1307) was to rebuild and convert the Norman castle into his most impressive stronghold in the east, but before it was completed an apparently insignificant event was to transform Cambridge and lead to eight centuries of intellectual glory.

In 1209 a handful of teachers and students fled from the university city of Oxford, where riots and intolerance had made their lives impossible. A few of them found their way to Cambridge and, though they lived in dank and mean lodgings, the beginnings of a great university were present.

In 1226 there was the first mention of a chancellor, and there were statutes of the university in about 1250. Cambridge was becoming a university in the fullest sense. There was an organised school, a number of Masters, there were arts and theological faculties, students came from distant regions, and there were privileges and a growing acceptance by the state. In 1318 Pope John XXII formally recognised the burgeoning academic community in a bull, calling Cambridge a *studium generale*. There was an urgent need for better lodgings for masters and scholars so halls and hostels were endowed. In 1284 Peterhouse, first of the colleges, was founded; by 1352 there were seven similar foundations, and by 1475 there were twelve. Colleges and university buildings proliferated – schools of divinity, arts and law appeared, as did a library.

From the founding of King's College in 1441 to that of Trinity College in 1546, the university grew and it gained an international reputation. Sir William Cecil, later Lord Burghley, Queen Elizabeth's chief minister and Chancellor of the University, gave Cambridge a new set of statutes which remained unchanged for 300 years. He insisted, for example, that all students be members of colleges – as they are still required to be today. Greater powers were granted to Masters and Fellows (Senior Members), and Cambridge found itself changing into an oligarchy.

Cambridge was very much Oliver Cromwell country for he was born in nearby Huntingdon in 1599, was an undergraduate at Sidney Sussex College, represented Cambridge in the Short and Long Parliaments and made the town the headquarters of the Eastern Association. In 1960 his head was finally buried, secretly, in the ante-chapel of his old college. Despite Cromwell's influence, many colleges remained royalist and sent much of their plate to aid the King.

Most colleges were founded as schools of theology but in 1750, under the influence of Sir Isaac Newton, who was Lucasian

Professor of Mathematics for thirty-three years, mathematics became compulsory and the main subject of study. Fifty years later, the range of subjects was revised and broadened; a classical tripos (the Cambridge name for an examination leading to a degree) was introduced in 1824, mathematics ceased to be compulsory in 1850, natural sciences were introduced in 1851, engineering in 1894, and all religious tests were abolished in 1871. Today, more than forty subjects are taught.

Following a Royal Commission in 1920, the faculties were re-organised. The university had to undertake all public teaching, with the colleges retaining responsibility for individual supervision of their students. Today, the university is a self-governing body that is responsible also for the conferring of degrees. Cambridge now has about 11,700 undergraduates and

about 5,800 graduates, with 11 per cent of the total coming from over a hundred different countries outside the United Kingdom. Only about one-third of applicants are admitted.

The colleges, as at Oxford, are totally independent of the university and are self-governing corporate bodies that own

Left: *The Fitzwilliam Museum - the treasure-house of the university*
Below: *The University Church of Great St Mary's, in the centre of Cambridge*

property and create income. They are responsible for admitting undergraduates, and for their accommodation and welfare. By adhering firmly to

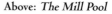

Above: *The Mill Pool*

their medieval collegiate system, the tradition of close contact between teacher and student is maintained and is an enviable source of intellectual vitality.

Much of Cambridge's charm stems from the intimate mingling of town and gown. Its river is crowded with punting students, townsfolk and tourists; the colourful marketplace is dominated by the University Church of Great St Mary's (1478), where degrees were conferred until the eighteenth century; and across the road is the Senate House (1722–30) designed by James Gibbs, where students are now awarded their degrees each June. Along Trumpington Street is one of the world's greatest university museums, the Fitzwilliam, named after the 7th Viscount Fitzwilliam, whose superb collection, bequeathed to Cambridge Unversity in 1816, forms the nucleus of this magnificent treasure house.

Today the City of Cambridge is a remarkable mixture of a small fenland market town, an internationally famed university and a world-renowned centre of twenty-first-century technology. However, its greatest glory must surely be the architectural splendour of the Cambridge colleges.

PETERHOUSE

Peterhouse, the oldest college in Cambridge, was founded in 1284 in two houses bought by Hugh de Balsham, Bishop of Ely, for a Master and fourteen 'worthy but impoverished Fellows' who were scholars or teachers and lived in the college but taught outside. It was not until the sixteenth century that paying students began to live in colleges. On his death in 1286, de Balsham bequeathed 300 marks to his scholars, who bought more land and built a hall, the only building to survive from the thirteenth century. It was heavily restored in the 1870s, when the oriel window was added. There are daisy tiles by William Morris in the Tudor fireplace and the windows by Morris, Burne-Jones and Madox Browne have some of the finest pre-Raphaelite stained glass in the country.

The scholars worshipped in St Peter's-without-Trumpington-Gate, which was rebuilt in 1340 and renamed St Mary the Less. But in 1628, under the mastership of Mathew Wren (uncle of Christopher), the original houses were demolished and the library and chapel were built. The west exterior of the chapel illustrates the transition from Gothic to Renaissance architecture that took place under the Stuarts. The chapel has a lovely ceiling with gilded suns and a beautiful wooden Gothic *pietà* behind the altar. In 1634 the Parliamentarians

destroyed 100 cherubim and angels and broke all the glass except the east window, a Crucifixion based on Rubens' *Le Coup de Lance*, which had been removed earlier and hidden. The eight side windows are by Professor Max Ainmüller of Munich (1855).

The fifteenth-century Old Court was classicised in the eighteenth century. A Master introduced deer into the Deer Park in the nineteenth century, but they died out in the 1930s. The Scholars' Garden is laid out in the style of the eighteenth-entury landscape artists. The modern William Stone building is called after a great college benefactor who was a scholar in 1875 and died in 1958, aged 101.

At the turn of the twentieth century, Peterhouse was the first college to have electricity. This created considerable anger among the Cambridge laundresses when smuts from the generator dirtied their washing on nearby Laundress Green.

Poet Thomas Gray ('Elegy Written in a Country Churchyard'), up from 1742 to 1756, was

terrified of fire and had an iron bar outside his window with a rope ladder to escape by. He was teased unmercifully. When a student jokingly shouted 'fire', Gray's 'delicate white nightcap ... appeared at the window, but finding the mistake, retired again to the couch.' When the Master dismissed this as 'boyish frolics', Gray moved to Pembroke College, but the iron bar is still outside his old window.

Henry Cavendish, at Peterhouse in the eighteenth century, measured the density of water and was the first person to weigh the earth at six thousand million million million tons. Other notable Peterhouse men include Charles Babbage, inventor of the first mechanical computer, Sir Frank Whittle, inventor of the jet engine, and Sir Christopher Cockerell, inventor of the hovercraft.

The Master's lodge, a beautiful Queen Anne house which was bequeathed to Peterhouse in 1726, is across the road from the college.

CLARE COLLEGE

Clare is the second oldest college in Cambridge. Richard de Badew, Chancellor of the University, founded University Hall in 1326, but it was a poor foundation owning only two chairs, one for the Master, the other for distinguished visitors, and it was soon in financial difficulties. In 1338 the college was refounded by Lady Elizabeth de Clare as Clare Hall (it did not become Clare College until 1856). Elizabeth was the granddaughter of Edward I and a wealthy woman with modern ideas. As well as housing a Master and nineteen Fellows, her hall was to provide free lodging and education for ten

century all the buildings were so dilapidated that it was decided to replace them.

Clare built its new court further away from the neighbouring King's College Chapel and nearer the river. A foundation-stone was laid on 16 May 1638, but the Civil War interrupted the building. The Parliamentarians took stone and brick from the building-site to fortify Cambridge Castle. Oliver Cromwell, as Lord Protector, eventually paid for these materials. Clare Court was not finished until 1719, eighty-one years after the foundation-stone was laid, and yet the buildings are so harmoniously

Hamburg was installed in 1971. The beautiful octagonal ante-chapel has a glazed timber lantern. The hall contains contemporary panelling by Cornelius Austin and a lovely plaster ceiling from 1870.

Clare has the oldest bridge now crossing the river and the first in classical style. Thomas Grumbold was paid 3 shillings (15 p) for the drawings in 1638. There are fourteen stone balls on the bridge; one has a segment missing. This was supposedly Grumbold's revenge for poor payment because the bridge will never actually be completed.

Beyond the river is the charming Fellows' Garden, redesigned in 1947 by a Fellow of the college. The Avenue, laid out in 1690, leads to Memorial Court, which was built in 1924 in memory of the members of the college killed in the First World War.

Thirkill Court, with Henry Moore's bronze Falling Warrior, commemorates men from the Second World War. The Forbes Mellon Library (by Sir Philip Dowson) was completed in 1988.

Hugh Latimer, the Protestant reformer burned at the stake in Oxford by Mary Tudor, Charles Townshend, the Chancellor of the Exchequer who imposed the taxes that precipitated the American War of Independence, and General Lord Cornwallis, who surrendered his army to the Americans at Yorktown in 1781, were all Clare men.

poor boys. The black surround with gold teardrops on the coat of arms is a mourning band; Lady Elizabeth had three husbands who all died before she was twenty-eight.

The original buildings were of clunch, a local building-material. In 1521 an extensive fire destroyed part of the court, which was rebuilt, but by the end of the sixteenth

proportioned it is said Clare looks 'more like a palace than a college'.

The chapel, begun in 1763, was designed by James Burrough and completed by James Essex with a barrel-vaulted ceiling. Above the altar is an *Annunciation* of 1763 by Cipriani, one of the founder members of the Royal Academy. A new organ by von Beckerath of

PEMBROKE COLLEGE

Pembroke College was founded in 1347 as 'The Hall of Marie Valence' by a French lady, Marie St Pol de Valence, the widowed Countess of Pembroke. Later it became Pembroke Hall and in 1856 Pembroke College. Aymer de Valence, Earl of Pembroke, was fifty years old when he married Marie, a girl of seventeen. Legend says she was a maid, wife and widow all in one day because her husband was killed in front of her in a friendly joust on their wedding day, but it is more likely that he died three years later of apoplexy.

The college statutes granted by Edward III contain two interesting clauses. Students of French birth, who had already studied at an English university, were to be given preference, and members of the college were to spy on their comrades and report them if they drank too much, quarrelled, were extravagant or visited disorderly houses.

The gatehouse is original and the oldest in Cambridge. It was refaced in the eighteenth century. Old Court was the smallest college court in the university, measuring only 55 feet (16.8m) by 95 feet (29m), but it was greatly enlarged in the nineteenth century when the south range of buildings was demolished.

In 1355 the Countess obtained a papal licence to build a chapel. This splendid building is now the Old Library. Its beautiful plaster ceiling, by Henry Doogood, a contemporary of Christopher Wren, shows the undersides of birds as they fly overhead. Ivy Court was built in the seventeenth century. Its south range Hitcham Building was paid for with money left to his old college by Sir Robert Hitcham, King's Sergeant, and was the only building erected in the university

during the Commonwealth.

Mathew Wren, a Fellow of Pembroke, Chaplain to Prince Charles (later Charles I) and Bishop of Ely, was imprisoned in the Tower of London for eighteen years by Oliver Cromwell. He vowed that on his safe release he would build a great chapel in his old college. He entrusted the work to his nephew Christopher, and Pembroke Chapel is the first completed work of Christopher Wren. It was consecrated on St Mathew's Day 1665, when Mathew Wren was eighty years old. The East end was extended by George Gilbert Scott in 1880. Above the altar is a Deposition after Barocci and beside it the chair of Nicholas Ridley, Bishop of London, who was burned for heresy by Mary Tudor at Oxford in 1555.

In the nineteenth century Alfred Waterhouse rebuilt the hall. He told the Fellows the old one was unsafe and then had to use gunpowder to demolish it. New buildings doubled the size of the college. Beside the Victorian library is a statue to William Pitt the Younger, who came up to Pembroke in 1773, aged fourteen. Pitt entered Parliament and became Britain's youngest Prime Minister when he was twenty-four years old. He introduced income tax as a 'temporary measure'!

GONVILLE AND CAIUS COLLEGE

The college has two names because it was founded twice. The first founder, Edmund Gonville, a parish priest from Norfolk, was granted a licence for Gonville Hall in 1348. He died three years later leaving a foundation but no money. His executor, William Bateman, Bishop of Norwich, moved Gonville Hall nearer to his own college of Trinity Hall, renaming it The Hall of the Annunciation of the Blessed Virgin Mary. He established Gonville Court in 1353 in two existing houses. The chapel was built in 1393 and the Master's lodge, the parlour, Old Hall (now a library) and the Old Library were completed by 1441. In the 1750s Gonville Court was given a classical facade.

The second founder, John Kees (latinised as Caius), came up in 1529 and studied medicine at Padua University from where he returned home in 1544. He was royal physician to Edward VI, Mary Tudor and Elizabeth I and was elected President of the Royal College of Physicians nine times. Dr Caius introduced the study of practical anatomy into England.

Saddened by the dilapidated state of his old college, he obtained a royal charter in 1557 to refound it as Gonville and Caius College. There is still a strong medical tradition.

The college was rededicated in 1558. Caius was elected Master. He accepted no payment but insisted on strange rules. The college was to admit no persons who were 'deaf, dumb, deformed, lame, chronic invalids or Welshmen'. The foundation-stone of Caius Court was laid on 5 May 1565 at 4 a.m. (sunrise), and Caius insisted on a three-sided court 'lest the air from being confined within a narrow space should become foul'. The college has three gates to symbolise the academic path. The entrance was the Gate of Humility. That is now in the Master's garden, but '*Humilitatis*' is carved beside the porters' lodge. The second gate in the centre of the college, and used regularly is the Gate of Virtutis (Virtue) - one of the first buildings in England in the Renaissance style. The third is the Gate of Honoris (Honour), under which students pass on their way to the Senate House to receive their degrees. This gate and its six sundials were restored in 1958 to commemorate the 400th anniversary of the refounding of the college.

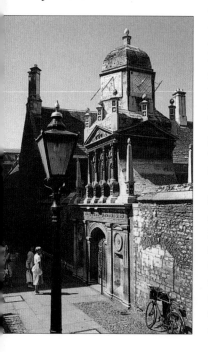

In 1637 the chapel was given its beautiful Jacobean cherub and sunray ceiling. The outside was refaced in stone in 1716.

The library and hall were designed by Anthony Salvin in 1854. On the wall near High Table is a small college flag flown at the South Pole by Dr Wilson in 1912 on Scott's ill-fated expedition. In 1869 Alfred Waterhouse demolished old buildings in Tree Court and rebuilt it in high-Victorian 'chateau' style.

Harvey Court (1961), across the river, designed by Sir Leslie Martin, is named after William Harvey, the great physiologist and physician to James I, who came up in 1593. He discovered the circulation of the blood, publishing his famous book on the subject in 1628.

Thomas Manning, a Caius mathematical tutor who brooded on 'the mysterious empire of China', learnt Chinese in Paris and went to Canton in 1806. He was the first Englishman to penetrate Lhasa and played chess with the Dalai Lama.

Dr Caius gave the college his astrolabe and caduceus, a silver wand 2½ feet (0.76 m) long with four entwined serpents, which is still carried in front of the Master at important college festivities.

TRINITY HALL

In the late 1340s, England was devastated by the Black Death. Nearly half the population perished, and William Bateman, Bishop of Norwich, lost almost 700 of his parish priests, which prompted him in 1350 to found 'The Hall of the Holy Trinity of Norwich' to educate students in the canon and civil law. Trinity Hall is still known as the lawyers' college and retains its title of 'Hall' which originally referred only to buildings, 'college' meaning scholars. In the nineteenth century other halls became colleges, but Trinity Hall was unable to do so because there already was a Trinity College.

The Principal Court was built gradually during the fourteenth century. When the Italianate look became fashionable in the eighteenth century, the whole court was given its classical appearance leaving one small medieval casement in the north-west corner. Much of the court was destroyed by fire in 1850 and was rebuilt by Salvin.

The chapel, Cambridge's smallest, was licensed in 1352; before this, colleges had used the nearest city church. The chapel and hall were modernised in the eighteenth century. The chapel ceiling bears coats of arms of college notables, including Stephen Gardiner, Bishop of Winchester, twice Master and the most powerful statesman in Mary

Tudor's England. The beautiful altarpiece is the *Presentation in the Temple* by Manzuoli.

Thomas Preston's brass is in the ante-chapel. He was the first college Master to marry when Elizabeth I gave them permission to do so. Two round, stained glass windows commemorate Robert Runcie, college dean from 1956 to 1960, who became Archbishop of Canterbury. The tiny fourteenth-century doorway led to the Master's lodge.

The library, with its Tudor brickwork and Elizabethan stepped gable, was built in the late sixteenth century. The door high in the wall was used by the Master, who had a walkway on top of a wall that crossed the court from his lodge opposite. The interior has Jacobean sloped reading-desks with shelves underneath; some books are still chained in the traditional manner to prevent their removal. One, written by Erasmus, was published in 1521 by the first Cambridge printer, John Siberch,

a German who borrowed £20 from the University Chest. He returned home without repaying his debt. In July 1971, when commemorating the printing of Cambridge's first book, the University Printer repaid the £20. (At five per cent compound interest he would have had to repay nearly £69 billion!)

In the parlour is a half-moon table at which Fellows sit to drink port. The open side has a railway with two trucks, worked by a wooden lever; bottles are placed in the trucks thus allowing the port to circle the table from right to left in the traditional manner.

The glorious herbaceous borders by the library and in the Fellows' Garden moved novelist Henry James to describe them as 'the prettiest corner of the world'.

Old 'Hall' men include Admiral Lord Howard of Effingham, the commander whose fleet defeated the Spanish Armada, and authors Robert Herrick ('Gather ye rosebuds while ye may') and J.B. Priestley.

CORPUS CHRISTI COLLEGE

Corpus Christi, uniquely amongst the colleges of Oxford and Cambridge, was founded by the townspeople, the members of the guilds of Corpus Christi and of the Blessed Virgin Mary. Its students were to 'be trained in academical learning' and to pray for the souls of the fraternity members for ever. Edward III granted the licence in 1352, and building began on a square site - the first college to have a quadrangle or 'court' as they are called in Cambridge. Old Court is one of Cambridge's oldest college buildings.

William Wilkins designed New Court, including a new chapel, where he is buried, in neo-Gothic style in the 1820s. New Court contains the library begun in 1376 but greatly enhanced by a bequest from Matthew Parker, Master 1544-53, who saved books and manuscripts from destruction following the Dissolution of the Monasteries. He was Archbishop of Canterbury under Elizabeth I. The books were to be locked with three keys held by the Master and two

century Gospel, believed to have been given to St Augustine by Pope Gregory, which is used at the enthronement of the Archbishop of Canterbury.

Corpus has the finest collection of pre-Reformation silver in Cambridge because, when most colleges gave their plate to the King or Parliament during the Civil War, Corpus distributed theirs amongst the Fellows who were given leave of absence and hid it until the Restoration. A drinking-horn which pre-dates the college is still used at college feasts.

Corpus men include Sir Nicholas Bacon and Matthew Parker, whose statues flank the chapel entrance doorway, Thomas Cavendish (1586), the second man to sail around the world, and the dramatists Christopher Marlowe and John Fletcher.

The college owns a portrait, discovered in an attic in the early twentieth century, of an unknown man dated 1585 with the legend: 'This was him in the 21st year of his age'. It is presumed to be Marlowe because in that year he was twenty-one.

Graduates of Corpus may dine and stay the night free in college four times each year.

Its original windows have rebated jambs and sills to hold oiled linen - used to keep out the cold east winds before glass was installed.

The large rooms had two windows, rush matting on the floor and were used as dormitories. They had study cubicles leading from them with one window each. A covered gallery led to St Bene't's Church, which was used as the college chapel until one was built in the sixteenth century. St Bene't's Saxon tower, of about 1025, is the oldest

building in Cambridge.

Fellows and inspected annually by the Masters of Gonville and Caius College and Trinity Hall. If certain numbers of manuscripts were missing, the whole collection and the college plate were to go to Caius, then to Trinity Hall and if they, too, mislaid books, the cycle started again. The scrutiny has only recently been discontinued. The books are priceless. Among them are: King Alfred's copy of *The Anglo-Saxon Chronicle*, a Psalter which belonged to Thomas à Becket and a sixth-

KING'S COLLEGE

In 1440 Henry VI, a young man of eighteen, established Eton College, and the next year founded the College of St Nicholas in Cambridge for twelve students. He began building Old Court and then decided on a much grander plan. Seventy scholars from Eton were to be able to complete their education here. Henry wanted a simple, enclosed court with the chapel as the north wall. He explained everything, even to the number and dimensions of the rooms, in his 'wille and entent' of 1448. The college was renamed The King's College of Our Lady and St Nicholas.

The site Henry chose for the new buildings was an important part of the medieval town, crossed by one of the main streets. The whole area was cleared, but in 1455 the Wars of the Roses intervened. Henry was deposed in 1461, and the site remained empty for almost 300 years.

Henry's greatest achievement must be King's College Chapel, the finest Gothic building in Europe and one of the best-known buildings in the world. On 25 July 1446, Henry laid the foundation-stone at the site of the high altar. The first external building-material was white magnesian limestone from Yorkshire. Work stopped on Henry's deposition and restarted later with buff-coloured oolitic limestone from Northampton-

shire. The change in the stone colour clearly demonstrates the extent of Henry VI's own building.

Work continued slowly under Edward IV and Richard III. Henry VII willed money for his own master mason, John Wastell, to complete the stonework. Wastell was probably responsible for the breath-taking fan vault – the largest and simplest in the world - with central bosses of alternating roses and portcullis, each weighing one ton. Tudor emblems proliferate in the ante-chapel: crowned roses, portcullises and fleurs-de-lis, and Henry VII's coat of arms supported by Welsh dragons and Richmond greyhounds.

Henry VIII gave the magnificent dark oak screen carrying his initials and those of Anne Boleyn, his Queen from 1533 to 1536. The organ case has

ornamentation from the original Thomas Dallam organ of 1605. Henry VIII sent his own glaziers to make the stained glass windows, paying for them himself.

A permanent exhibition in the northern side-chapels, entitled 'King's: The Building of a Chapel', shows why and how the chapel was built.

The Adoration of the Magi, which was given to the college by A.E. Allnatt in 1961, was painted by Rubens in eight days in 1634 for the White Nuns at Louvain in Belgium. The floor-level at the east end of the chapel was lowered so that this spectacular gift could stand above the altar without hiding the great east window.

King's has a world-famous choir of sixteen choristers and fourteen undergraduates, which sings at college services during

the term. Since 1928 the Festival of Nine Lessons and Carols has been broadcast around the world from the chapel every Christmas Eve. The small choristers wear Eton collars and top hats as they

walk in a crocodile from their school to the chapel for choir practice.

The chapel was completed in 1536, and the college undertook no more major building for almost 200 years. In 1724 James Gibbs designed the Fellows' Building. Its foundation stone was a huge stone deeply cut by masons working on the chapel who abandoned their work after Henry VI's deposition.

Almost a hundred years later the new bridge over the Cam was built and the college held a competition to select an architect to complete Front Court. The winner, William Wilkins, designed the neo-Gothic south range with the hall, senior combination room and library as well as the

delicate stone screen and gatehouse which separates the college from King's Parade. The fountain, with Henry VI's statue above it, was placed in the centre of Front Court in 1879. Henry VI's original Old Court was bought by the university in 1829 and is now the Registry, administrative headquarters of the university.

For 400 years, King's admitted only Etonians, who enjoyed special privileges: they were awarded degrees without sitting university examinations and were not subject to the authority of the University Proctors (Fellows responsible for discipline). In 1873 non-Etonians were admitted, and the first non-Etonian Fellow elected.

Rupert Brooke, First World War poet, was an undergraduate and Fellow of King's, living for a time in the vicarage at nearby Grantchester, and writer E.M. Forster was an undergraduate and honorary Fellow. Maynard Keynes, the economist, studied at King's and later became the college bursar.

QUEENS' COLLEGE

The true founder of Queens' was Rector Andrew Dokett, whose likeness is carved on the keystone above the Gate Tower. Dokett founded St Bernard's College in 1446 for a President and four Fellows - Queens' still has a President rather than the more usual Master. In 1448, Margaret of Anjou obtained permission from her husband, Henry VI, to refound and rename St Bernard's as 'The Queen's College of St Margaret and St Bernard' to 'laud and honneure of Sexe feminine'. In 1465 Elizabeth of Woodville, Queen of Edward IV and former Lady of the Bed-chamber to Queen Margaret, became Patroness, giving the college its statutes and the green border to the Anjou coat of arms. The support of both queens is acknowledged in the spelling *Queens'*, with the apostrophe after the *s*.

Old Court, completed in 1449, is a pictures-que, almost unaltered example of medieval brickwork, containing everything essential to a college - chapel, library, hall and living-area in a single, confined space. The dial of 1733 is one of the finest exam-ples of a sundial in Britain and one of the few moondials in the world. The hall was classicised

in the eighteenth century and 'restored' in the nineteenth with mantle tiles by William Morris, Burne-Jones and Rossetti and over 900 gilded lead stars on the walls and ceiling.

Erasmus's Tower in the corner of Pump Court is near rooms he used between 1510 and 1514 when he taught Greek in the university. Erasmus was unim-pressed with the climate, wine and the high costs in Cambridge but thought the women were 'the kissing kind'. Cloister Court contains the beautiful late sixteenth-century Long Gallery of the President's lodge above the fifteenth-century cloisters. For many years it was covered in plaster, which was removed in 1911 to reveal the Tudor half-timbering. The famous wooden bridge, popularly called the

screws or bolts at its main joints.

Walnut Tree Court (the present tree is a descendant of a much older one) with its Jacobean range and Victorian chapel leads to the Erasmus

Mathematical Bridge, was built in 1749 and rebuilt of teak in 1905 to the original design. The belief that the bridge had no nails is incorrect, it always had iron

Building in Friars' Court, designed by Sir Basil Spence in 1960. The first modern building on the Backs, it aroused considerable controversy.

St Catharine's College

In 1473 Robert Woodlark, third Provost of King's, founded Katharine Hall (renamed St Catharine's College in 1860) for a Master and three Fellows who were to study nothing but 'philosophy and sacred theology' and were to pray for the souls of their benefactors for ever. The college is named after Catharine of Alexandria. Condemned to be crucified on a wheel, it miraculously broke when she touched it and eventually she was beheaded. The catharine-wheel firework is named after her.

entrance to Katharine Hall was on Milne Street, now Queens' Lane, and the original buildings were of clunch. By the seventeenth century they were dilapidated, and it was decided to rebuild the college. The west and south ranges of the Principal Court were completed by 1695. The chapel, finished in 1704 under Master Sir William Dawes, contains a touching memorial to his young wife. The chapel was built on the site of Thomas Hobson's livery stables, where the phrase 'Hobson's choice'

Gothicised in 1868 to complement the new oriel window in the hall. The court was greatly admired by John Ruskin for its dark-coloured bricks. In 1965 King's and St Catharine's collaborated in a major rebuilding scheme which included a new hall for St Catharine's.

James Shirley, poet and dramatist, came up in the early seventeenth century, and St Catharine's can claim one of the youngest undergraduates. William Wotton, born in 1666, knew Latin, Greek and Hebrew when he was six, came up aged nine and was made a Fellow of the Royal Society at twenty-one. John Addenbrooke was admitted to

Woodlark gave his books to the library, insisting on strict rules: they were to be examined annually and none was to leave the college except to be bound or repaired. Fellows could work by candlelight, but visitors had to leave the library at sunset. The

originated. Hobson insisted his horses were used in strict rotation: 'My choice or no choice.'

James Essex designed the Ramsden Building for the southeast side of the court in 1757. The north side windows were

St Catharine's in 1697 to read medicine. On his death in 1719 he left £4,500 to found the famous Addenbrooke's Hospital in Cambridge. He is buried in the chapel, and the college has his medicine chest, which he willed to them.

JESUS COLLEGE

When John Alcock, Bishop of Ely, visited the twelfth-century Benedictine nunnery of St Radegund in 1496 he found it impoverished. Only two nuns were left and one was 'infamis' so he obtained a licence from Henry VII to suppress the nunnery and establish 'The College of the Blessed Virgin Mary, St John the Evangelist and the Glorious Virgin St Radegund', known always as Jesus College. Alcock built a fine gate-tower with his statue in the centre and above it his rebus – a cockerel standing on a globe – which is repeated throughout the college. The gate-tower is approached by a long, narrow high-walled path called 'The Chimney'.

The conventual buildings were adapted for the college. The nuns' cloisters were given open arches in 1768. Three early English arches on the east side of Cloister Court were the entrance to the nuns' chapter-house which was destroyed by Alcock. The arches were hidden under plaster and only discovered in 1893. Inside the entrance to Cloister Court is a recess low down in the wall called 'the rota' where nuns could get a mug of small ale from the pantry. The hall above the kitchens was the nuns' refectory and has been used continuously as a dining chamber for over 800 years.

The nuns' church became the college chapel - the oldest building in any Cambridge college. Alcock demolished the aisles, and the west end was incorporated into the Master's lodge. It has a fine early thirteenth-century choir, although the screen and stalls are Victorian. The bench end of the Master's Stall is original and

shows Alcock praying. In the nineteenth century, Pugin designed the chancel roof, William Morris the nave and tower ceilings and Burne-Jones some of the glass. The south transept has a memorial to Archbishop Thomas Cranmer, Jesus undergraduate, later Fellow and first Protestant Archbishop of Canterbury, who was burned at the stake by Mary Tudor in 1556 after he repudiated his earlier acknowledgement of the Catholic doctrine. Nearby is a memorial to Samuel Taylor Coleridge, who came up in 1791 but left without taking his degree.

Chapel Court (1885) had a south range added in 1928 with a coat of arms and supporting angels carved by Eric Gill. The nuns of St Radegund are still buried outside the east end of the chapel.

The modern North Court, opened in 1965, was where Prince Edward had his rooms when he came up in 1983.

The Old Library has an autographed copy of the first edition of the first bible printed in America. Printed in Cambridge, Massachusetts, in 1663 in Algonquin, it was translated by Jesus man John Eliot who sailed to the New World to convert the North American Indians to Christianity.

CHRIST'S COLLEGE

William Byngham established the small college of God's-house in about 1437 on a site near the river to encourage men to read for the lesser degree of Master of Grammar and so replace the huge numbers of teachers killed by the Black Death. It was the forerunner of teacher-training colleges. When Henry VI began building King's College, God's-house was forced to move to its present site. Head of the house was John Syclyng, whose friend, Bishop John Fisher, was chaplain and confessor to the Lady Margaret Beaufort, mother of Henry VII. Fisher persuaded her to 'finish and establish God's-house'. The royal charter was granted on 1 May 1505, and the college flag is always flown on that day. The college was dedicated to Jesus Christ and was known thereafter as Christ's College. John Syclyng continued as Master.

Some of the buildings in First Court date from God's-house, but the remainder and the Great Gate were completed before the foundress died. The court is not square because it follows the street line. Due to the rise in the street level over 400 years, the bottom ofthe wooden entrance gates has had to be removed. In the eighteenth century the buildings were classicised and refaced. Lady Margaret's statue above the gate shows her

holding a bible; below her and above the door to the Master's lodge, are the Tudor rose, the Beaufort portcullis and her coat of arms supported by the mythological yales which are also on St John's Gate.

The chapel belonged to God's-house but was enlarged in 1506 and panelled in 1702. It has the original chestnut ceiling and some of the oldest stained glass in Cambridge. Near the altar is a splendid double memorial (1684) to inseparable Fellows Sir John Finch and Sir Thomas Baines. Baines died in Constantinople, and Finch had his body embalmed and brought home so they could be buried together. John Syclyng's memorial brass is

inside the altar rails.

The hall was restored in 1876 using some of the old linenfold panelling. The portraits there include John Milton, who came up in 1628, Charles Darwin (1825) and Field Marshal Jan Smuts (1891), an Honorary Fellow. Milton was a pale and delicate young man, and other students nicknamed him 'the lady of Christ's'.

The Fellows' Building of 1642 is one of the earliest examples of classical architecture in Cambridge. The central gates lead to the glorious Fellows' Garden, laid out in the early nineteenth century. It has several beehives, an eighteenth-century bathing pool and Milton's mulberry tree - probably planted by order of James I to encourage the silk industry - under which Milton reputedly sat to write poetry.

The dramatically modern New Court was designed by Sir Denys Lasdun and begun in 1966.

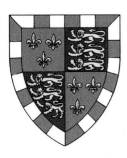

ST JOHN'S COLLEGE

Lady Margaret Beaufort, mother of Henry VII, had already founded Christ's College and established a lectureship in divinity when Bishop John Fisher, her confessor and a leading figure in the university, persuaded her to found a college on the site of a thirteenth-century hospital run by the Monks of St John. Lady Margaret died in 1509 before work had begun but left a codicil in her will empowering her executors to carry out her design. The Charter of the College of St John the Evangelist was granted on 9 April 1511.

The Gate Tower of red brick dressed with stone (1516) has St John's statue (1662) with his symbolic eagle at his feet. It replaces the original, removed during the Civil War and subsequently lost. Lady Margaret's coat of arms is supported by mythical yales with goats' heads, antelopes' bodies and elephants' tails. Their horns move independently. The crowned Tudor rose and Beaufort portcullis are surrounded by daisies (marguerites for 'Margaret') and forget-me-nots symbolising her motto *Souvent me Souvient*.

The linenfold doors were restored in 1666 after the gatehouse withstood a Cromwellian siege. St John's still celebrates Oak-apple Day, 29 May, the restoration of the monarchy, with a feast and 'oaken boughs' in the hall.

First Court (1511) is a fine example of Tudor brickwork. It

incorporates the Hospital chapel, whose foundation stones can still be seen on the lawn. When the south side was being classicised, a hunted stag was killed in the doorway of 'G' staircase. Workmen carved 'Stag. Nov 15, 1777' above the lintel. Poet William Wordsworth lived on 'F' staircase from 1787 to 1791.

Gilbert Scott designed the chapel (1869) with a spire, but an Old Johnian promised £1,000 annually for five years to build a tower instead. After two payments, he died in a railway accident, and the college was obliged to fund the remainder. Each Ascension Day at noon, the chapel choir sings hymns from the roof of the tower. The antechapel contains the memorial tomb of Hugh Ashton (executor to Lady Margaret). On top he lies in academic robes; beneath he is an emaciated, shrouded corpse. There is also a statue to Johnian William Wilberforce, who helped abolish the slave trade.

Second Court (1602), paid for mainly by Mary, Countess of Shrewsbury - whose statue overlooks the court - contains the Fellows' panelled combination room. At 93 feet (28.3 m) it is the longest room in Cambridge and is still lit only by

New Court is a masterpiece of Gothic Revival architecture. Its central tower, with battlements and turrets, is traditionally known as 'The Wedding Cake'. Linking New Court to the older courts is the equally picturesque 'Bridge of Sighs' (1831). Designed by Henry Hutchinson, the only similarity of the bridge to its Venetian namesake is that both are covered. In 1956, undergraduate pranksters punted a small car up the river and hung it from the bridge.

Cripps Court, constructed of Portland stone in 1967 for about £1.5 million, was awarded the RIBA Bronze Medal. This most modern court leads to the 'School of Pythagoras'. Built about 1200, it is the oldest domestic building in the county.

The Lady Margaret Boat Club, founded in 1825, is the oldest college club on the River Cam. Its oarsmen wear scarlet jackets, which gave rise to the name 'Blazer'. They challenged Oxford to a boat race in 1829 and so began the annual University Boat Race rowed on the River Thames in London.

candle-light. During the Second World War, the D-Day Landings were partly planned in this room. In 1824 St John's began building beyond the river.

MAGDALENE COLLEGE

The monasteries were anxious that their young men should be properly supervised and housed whilst studying at Cambridge so in 1428 the Abbott of Crowland bought two 'messuages' (plots of land) and began Monks' Hostel. Its statutes displayed a realistic view of university life – 'students of this College are to visit taverns less often than other students'. The abbeys of Ely, Ramsey and Walden joined the venture and in the late 1400s began building the first court. Money was provided by Henry, 2nd Duke of Buckingham, and the college became known as Buckingham College.

At the Dissolution, Henry VIII gave the college to his Lord Chancellor, Thomas, Baron Audley of Walden, who refounded it in 1542 as 'The College of St Mary Magdalene' (pronounced 'Maudlin'). His descendants still have the right to select new masters for the college. Audley died young and left his college poor. It could barely support four Fellows – Audley wanted eight – and could not afford to finish the court. Audley's son-in-law, the Duke of Norfolk, gave the college £40 a year until they had 'builded a quadrant' but was subsequently beheaded so the court was not finished until 1580. It is brick-faced clunch, the local building-stone, but was covered with

cement in the 1700s. This was stripped off in 1950 to reveal the lovely original warm brick, and coats of arms of the four Abbeys were placed over the south side doorways.

The chapel was central to college life. The monks began building theirs forty years before they built a hall. The interior was classicised in the mid-eighteenth century, but this process was reversed in the 1840s. The east window is by Pugin. The modern bronze statuette outside the chapel doorway is of Henry VI aged seven, his age when Monks' Hostel was founded.

A small hall was built in 1519 and was enlarged and altered in 1714 when the unique double staircase to the gallery was installed. It is the last hall in Cambridge to be lit only by candle-light.

The Pepys Building in Second Court houses Samuel Pepys' own library, left by him on his death in 1703, first to his nephew and then to his old college 'intire in one body ... for the benefit of posterity.' The inscription 'Bibliotheca Pepysiana 1724' refers to the year the library was installed. The bequest insisted the library should be complete. No books were to be added or removed. There are 3,000 volumes housed in Pepys' own library table and twelve red oak

presses designed by Pepys himself, probably the first bookcases ever to keep books behind glass. The books are catalogued by size, the smallest to the largest, with small books standing on wooden,

book-shaped blocks to make all the books level. The gift included Pepys' diary, bound in six volumes and written in shorthand. The Revd John Smith of St John's College spent three laborious years deciphering the diary only to find at the end that a complete key to the shorthand code existed in the library. The Fellows' Garden contains a fifteenth-century fishpond and a Victorian pets' cemetery.

Among the courts across the road from the main college are Benson, designed by Lutyens, called after Master A.E. Benson who wrote the words of 'Land of Hope and Glory', and Mallory, after George L. Mallory who perished a few feet from the summit of Mount Everest in 1924.

In 1988 Magdalene became the last male college to admit women students. At the beginning of term the men wore black armbands and flew the college flag at half mast!

TRINITY COLLEGE

The College of the Holy and Undivided Trinity, the largest of the Oxbridge colleges, has nurtured many leading intellectuals, including thirty-one Nobel Prize winners. Henry VIII founded it in 1546 as one of his last acts - he died five weeks later. Henry amalgamated the two small colleges of King's Hall and Michaelhouse - both over 200 years old - giving his new college substantial endowments from the monasteries he had dissolved. He wished to be remembered as the

him are the coats of arms of Edward III, founder of King's Hall, and his six sons. The plain shield belongs to William of Hatfield, who died in infancy. Nearby is an apple-tree which was planted in 1954, a descendant of the tree whose apple fell on Isaac Newton at Woolsthorpe in Lincolnshire and prompted him to experiment with gravitation.

Mary Tudor began building the chapel in 1554 in memory of her father. The interior was panelled in the eighteenth century, when

Laureate, Francis Bacon, philosopher and essayist and Roubiliac's magnificent representation of Isaac Newton holding a prism in his hand.

Elizabeth I appointed Thomas Nevile as Master of Trinity in 1593. A wealthy man with strong views on architecture, he was the inspiration behind the Great Court which, with its 2 acres (0.8 ha) of lawns and pathways, is the largest court at Oxford or Cambridge. Nevile demolished unwanted buildings, rebuilding a single court in Tudor-Gothic style with a splendid central fountain and moving the clock tower, the oldest surviving building in the college, into line with the chapel. The eighteenth-century clock, which replaces an earlier one, strikes the hours twice, first with a low note, then a higher one. It is the clock 'with a male and female voice' of Wordsworth's 'Prelude'. Traditionally, undergraduates attempt to run around the Great Court while the clock strikes twelve twice - 380 yards (347.5 m) in 43 seconds.

greatest founder of the greatest college.

Henry's early seventeenth-century statue stands on the Great Gate, completed in 1535 for King's Hall. He is holding a chair leg in his right hand instead of the expected sceptre; this was a student's joke from the late nineteenth century. Below

the baldachin painting of *St Michael and the Devil* was commissioned from Benjamin West. One of the nineteenth-century stained glass windows shows Mary Tudor holding a model of the chapel. The ante-chapel contains statues of famous Trinity men, including Alfred, Lord Tennyson, the Poet

Nevile's fine Elizabethan hall is modelled on the hall of

London's Middle Temple. It is the largest hall in Cambridge and has a hammer-beam roof, a minstrel's gallery and a roof lantern now covering the hole through which smoke from a central brazier could escape. The west oriel window contains coats of arms of members of the royal family, including the Prince of Wales, who came up to Trinity in 1967. Amongst portraits of Trinity men are Lord Byron, John Dryden and Lord Rutherford, who split the atom for the first time at the Cavendish Laboratory in Cambridge in 1932.

Elegant, cloistered Nevile's Court was paid for by Thomas Nevile and completed in 1612, three years before his death. Its north cloister is where Newton stamped his foot and timed the returning echo to calculate the speed of sound for the first time.

In 1673 Master Isaac Barrow convinced the Fellows of the need for a new library and persuaded his friend Christopher Wren to design it and supervise the building work for nothing. The library, completed in 1695, is the best example of classical architecture in the university. The statues on the external balustrade, representing Divinity, Law, Physic and Mathematics, are by Gabriel Cibber. Wren designed the book cases, stools and revolving reading-tables. The beautiful limewood carvings are by Grinling Gibbons. Thorvaldsen's

marble statue of Lord Byron was originally offered to Westminster Abbey for the Poets' Corner but was refused by the Dean because of Byron's questionable morals. When Byron was up at Trinity, undergraduates were not allowed to keep dogs. He decided to have a tame bear instead so that it could 'sit for its Fellowship'. The books in the Wren Library are the college collection as it was in 1820 with a small number of later additions. The oldest is an eighth-century manuscript of the Epistles of St Paul; one of the newest is the original manuscript of A.A. Milne's *Winnie the Pooh*. Milne and his son, Christopher Robin, were both Trinity men. There is also a first edition of Newton's *Principia Mathematica*, containing his own margin corrections for the second edition, and John Milton's shorter poems in his own handwriting, the only known

example of it.

Beyond the library is the River Cam and the Backs, a lovely, world-renowned expanse of trees, lawns, pastures and gardens behind the riverside colleges, which are particularly beautiful when carpeted by springtime crocuses, daffodils and tulips and when the leaves change to their spectacular autumnal colours.

EMMANUEL COLLEGE

Sir Walter Mildmay, Chancellor of the Exchequer to Elizabeth I, founded Emmanuel College in 1584 on the site of a former Dominican friary he had bought for £550. Mildmay, a man of Puritan sympathies, wanted his college to be a 'seed-plot of learned men' for the new Protestant church. Ralph Symons adapted the existing buildings. To underline the changes in religious thinking, the friary church became the dining-hall and the refectory the college chapel running on a north-south axis. This is now the Old Library. The founder was present in 1588 at the Feast of Dedication in the newly white-washed hall. The meal included 'venison from two does, and a cragg of sturgeon'.

Brick Building, now called Old Court, was built in 1633 when John Harvard was an undergraduate. He sailed to New England and died ofconsumption in 1638, leaving half his estate and 320 books to found a 'schoale at Newetowne', which was called after him and became America's first university. A third of the first hundred British graduates to settle in New England were from Emmanuel. The chapel has a plaque in Harvard's memory.

Master William Sancroft asked Christopher Wren to design a new, properly orientated college chapel, which was completed in 1677 with cloisters and a gallery at the west end and a pedestal clock and cupola above them. The woodwork (Cornelius Austin) and the plaster ceiling, decorated with fruit, leaves and flowers (James Grove), are original. The cut-glass chandelier and altar painting of *The Return of the Prodigal* by Jacopo Amigoni were given in the 1730s.

Front Court was re-built in the eighteenth century. The hall was refaced and decorated, and a new entrance front was designed by James Essex. New Court, actually the original court of the college, was given a neo-Gothic range in 1824, and its Herb Garden was planted in 1961.

Emmanuel has beautiful gardens. The pond in the Paddock was formerly the monks' fishpond. It is still well stocked with fish and is home to a large and varied population of ducks. Beyond it is The Hostel, built on the foundations of the monastic brew house.

SIDNEY SUSSEX COLLEGE

Lady Frances Sidney, Countess of Sussex, died in 1589, leaving £5,000, her plate and other effects to found a new college at Cambridge called 'The Ladie ffrauncis Sydney Sussex Colledge'. She was childless but 'such learned persons who receive their Breeding in her Foundation may be termed her Issue'. Her executors attempted to purchase the site of a Franciscan friary given to Trinity College by Henry VIII. Trinity objected, and it took a strongly worded letter from Elizabeth I to change their minds. The Queen granted a charter in 1594, and work began in 1595. Trinity had dismantled most of the site for their own buildings; only the partly demolished refectory was left. Ralph Symons, the builder, divided this into two floors with a chapel underneath and library above. Two years later, Hall Court, containing the kitchen, with the Master's lodge above it, the hall and the buttery, was ready for occupation.

In 1627 Sir Francis Clerke gave money for four fellowships, eight scholarships and additional buildings, thus completing Chapel Court, a second three-sided court to the south. James Essex, who was asked to design a

new chapel in 1774, produced four plans before they were approved. The chapel was altered and lengthened in 1912 and given elaborate oak-panelled walls and a variegated marble floor. The altarpiece of *The Holy Family* by Giovanni Battista Pittoni was bought in 1783 for

twenty guineas. The fine gardens were laid out in the eighteenth century.

By the beginning of the nineteenth century the buildings were seriously dilapidated. Jeffry Wyatt (who became Sir Jeffry Wyattville) removed the classical gateway, replacing it with a new porters' lodge and tower. He covered the red brick buildings with Roman cement, adding a porch and bell-turret to the chapel, and gables and battlements in the Gothic manner. Cloister Court, with its arcaded walk, was completed in the 1890s and Garden Court in 1923.

The most famous undergraduate at Sidney must be Oliver Cromwell. He came up on

23 April 1616, the day William Shakespeare died, but left Cambridge after one year to support his family following his father's death. He became Lord Protector of England after the execution of Charles I. At the Restoration, Cromwell's body was exhumed, hanged and beheaded. His head was impaled on a pole on Westminster Hall. Twenty years later it blew down in a great storm. It was presented to the college by Dr H.N.S. Wilkinson in 1960 and was buried in a secret place in the ante-chapel in the presence of the Master and two Fellows. A commemorative plaque is nearby. In the hall is a pastel portrait of Cromwell by Samuel Cooper which, like Sir Peter Lely's famous portrait, shows Cromwell 'warts and all'. Cromwell's college did not share his political sympathies. During the Civil War, Sidney sent £100 to help the King, and the Master was imprisoned for failing to support the Parliamentarians.

DOWNING COLLEGE

Downing College was founded by Sir George Downing, the 3rd baronet, with wealth left by his grandfather, who served both Cromwell and Charles II and who built Number 10 Downing Street, home of British prime ministers. Sir George was born in 1685. His mother died when he was three, and he lived with his aunt and cousin Mary whom he married when she was thirteen and he was fifteen. They were too young to live together so after the ceremony he went on the Grand Tour for two years. In 1703 Mary became Maid of Honour to Queen Anne against her husband's wishes. He never forgave her and never lived with her. In 1717 an Act of Parliament gave him legal sanction to live apart from her without being divorced.

Sir George would never have a legitimate heir so he left his estates to his cousin Jacob. If Jacob died without issue they were to go to three other cousins. If they all died childless the estates were to found a college at Cambridge.

George died in 1749 and Jacob in 1764, all the other heirs having predeceased him. The college should have been founded, but Jacob's widow, Lady Margaret, refused to relinquish the estates. After thirty-one years of legal battles, Lady Margaret lost but was allowed to keep the estates during her lifetime. When she died her second husband fought to keep the money. In 1800 the Court of Chancery decided in favour of Sir George's will, and George III granted Downing College a royal charter.

The original fortune was sadly depleted so Downing began as a poor college. Land was sold to pay for the building. This is now the Downing Site, containing university museums and laboratories. The first stone was laid in 1807. Architect William Wilkins adopted a neo-Grecian style because George III dis-approved of Gothic revival. Downing has no courts. Wilkins built an American-style campus some years before the first campus was designed at the University of Virginia. The east and west ranges have Ionic colonnades with the Master's lodge in one, the hall in the other. Four blocks were added in 1932. In 1956 the north range was completed, and the chapel by A.T. Scott was consecrated. Professor W.G. Howell's design for the senior combination room in 1969 won a number of architectural prizes. The Howard Building of 1987, paid for by college member Dr Alan Howard and designed by Quinlan Terry, was also widely acclaimed.

GIRTON COLLEGE

In December 1867, a committee of eminent men and women, who were all conscious of the need to promote the higher education of women, met to explore the possibility of founding a women's college. Two years later, Emily Davies, relying heavily on the committee's support, established Britain's first residential college for women at Hitchin in Hertfordshire. It was called Hitchin College and opened with six students. Cambridge lecturers travelled to Hitchin, but the disadvantages of being so far away from the university were obvious and, as the lease on the original building was due to expire, it was decided to transfer this fledgling college to Cambridge, but not into Cambridge. Sixteen acres (6.5 ha) of land was bought at Girton, 2½ miles (4 km) north of the city centre, 'near enough for male lecturers to visit but far enough away to discourage male students from doing the same'. The college now sits in 50 acres (20 ha) of immaculate grounds.

Alfred Waterhouse designed the first buildings in red brick Tudor-Gothic style in the traditional college form with a chapel and hall but he introduced the idea of bed-sitting-rooms being on corridors instead of the usual vertical staircases. In October 1873, the ladies moved into Girton College, named after the village that gave them a home, with Emily Davies as the first Head or Mistress. The imposing gatehouse was designed in 1887 by Paul Waterhouse in his father's Tudor-Gothic style with one octagonal corner-tower. Grandson Michael completed Woodlands Court in the 1930s.

The chapel is an integral part of the original buildings. It has a fine stained glass window by L.C. Evetts with symbolism from The Book of Revelation, which was installed in 1953. The lovely kneelers were embroidered by past Girton students to commemorate the centenary of the college foundation. The organ was rebuilt in1974.

Girton has one of the larger college working libraries in Cambridge with over 95,000 books. In 1967 the main library building was enlarged. Girton was granted full collegiate status in 1948, when women became full members of the university. In

that year Queen Elizabeth the Queen Mother became the first woman to be awarded a Cambridge degree when she was made an Honorary Doctor of Law.

To celebrate its centenary in 1969 Girton fmally moved into the city by opening a satellite court near the University Library. Wolfson Court is designed as an inward-looking Scandinavian-type five-court complex. One hundred and ten years after its foundation Girton admitted male students.

NEWNHAM COLLEGE

Newnham, the second women's college to be founded at Cambridge and still only for women, is situated in and named after Newnham village, 'a four-minute bike ride from the centre of the town'. The college had a modest beginning. In 1871, concern for

the lack of female opportunity in higher education prompted Henry Sidgwick, Fellow of Trinity College, to rent No. 74 Regent Street to provide lodgings for five women from outside Cambridge. They were supervised by Anne Jemima Clough. The present site was acquired, and Newnham Hall opened in 1875 with Miss Clough as the Principal. Architect Basil Champneys designed attractive, warm red brick buildings in the William-and-Mary style with Dutch gables and sparkling white woodwork. Old Hall was completed in 1875, and in 1880 Sidgwick Hall was built.

Miss Clough wanted 'her girls' to be inconspicuous in behaviour and appearance. They were always chaperoned. When attending university lectures, women sat at one side of the hall, men at the other. One lecturer insisted on addressing his entirely female audience as 'gentlemen'. The women played hockey but had to wear long skirts and were hidden from passers-by. A visiting team brought a male umpire who was asked to leave before the ladies went onto the pitch.

In 1881 Cambridge University allowed women to sit the tripos examination – so-called because originally the examiner sat on a three-legged stool – but they were not awarded degrees. This date is celebrated annually at Newnham's Commemoration Dinner. Cambridge men were shocked in 1890 when a woman gained the highest marks in the mathematical tripos – maths was considered too intellectually testing for women.

Clough Hall, the Pfeiffer Building, the Kennedy Building and Peile Hall were all completed by 1910. The buildings are set round three sides of the large, formal gardens. Students at Newnham are allowed on the grass, unlike the older colleges where only Fellows may walk on the lawns in the courts.

In 1919 Newnham received its charter and statutes. Women were admitted to the 'titles of degrees' in 1921, but it was not until 1948 that women became full members of the university. The first college building in Cambridge to be designed by a woman was the Fawcett Building at Newnham by Elizabeth Whitworth Scott in 1938. The Principal's lodge, by Louis Osman in 1958, resembles a classical villa with a central court walled with sheets of plate glass decorated with abstract patterns in aluminium and coloured glass, symbolising the four seasons. They are by Geoffrey Clarke, who also planned windows in the new Coventry Cathedral. When fitted, they were said to be the largest sheets of plate glass in the world.

The library, given to the college by Mr and Mrs Yates Thompson in 1897, was enlarged by Christopher Grillet in 1961, with a further striking extension - of grey brick with vertical red bands in 1981. Newnham has the largest undergraduate college library in Cambridge. The Y-shaped Strachey Building, also by Grillet, was opened in 1968.

Newnham has no chapel because it was founded by an agnostic as a non-denominational college. It does have the second-longest corridor in Europe, linking all parts of the college. The longest corridor is reputedly in Germany.

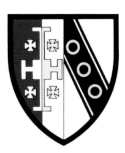

SELWYN COLLEGE

Selwyn College was founded by public subscription in 1882 in memory of George Augustus Selwyn, who rowed in the Cambridge crew in the first Varsity Boat Race in 1829 and who became the first Bishop of New Zealand, helping also to create that dominion. He returned to England as Bishop of Lichfield. Following his death in 1878, a committee proposed that a new Cambridge college would be a fitting memorial to him. The foundation charter specified that the college should 'make provision for those who intend to serve as missionaries overseas and ... educate the sons of clergymen.' Membership was originally restricted to baptised Christians.

University education was expensive. Selwyn was to be a college for poorer students, so charges were low. Undergraduates paid £27 a term for food, lodging, lectures and tuition with a small surcharge for medics, scientists and engineers. Selwyn began as a public hostel. It became an Approved Foundation in 1926 and was granted full collegiate status in 1958, admitting women in 1976.

In 1879 the founders bought 6 acres (2.4 ha) of farmland from Corpus Christi College for £6,111 9s. 7d., and elected a Master. Sir Arthur Blomfield designed the first buildings in Tudor-Gothic style. The first undergraduates arrived in 1882. Strangely, the first recorded motion of the Selwyn Debating Society in 1883 was disapproval of 'further operations in the matter of the Channel Tunnel'.

The chapel was built in 1895

before the dining-hall because it was deemed to be more important. It has a fine east window by Kempe, partly paid for by donations from New Zealand, and two bells, the louder one given by Prime Minister Gladstone, friend of the first Master.

The third Master, A.F. Kirkpatrick, an ex-seafaring man, shouted at students from his window like a captain on the bridge of his ship. He found standing difficult so remained seated for the loyal toast. Senior members of Selwyn still do this in his memory.

The south range and Jacobean hall were built in 1901. Wood-

work at the west end of the hall comes from the eighteenth-century English church of St Mary in Rotterdam which was demolished in 1913.

The library, completed in 1929 as a memorial to college men and servants killed in the First World War, houses a fine collection of sixteenth- and seventeenth-century books.

Cripps Court, designed by Gordon Woollatt in 1969, was funded by donations from former Selwyn men and money from the Cripps Foundation.

During the Second World War, Royal Air Force cadets drilled in the courts, the porters' lodge became an air raid wardens' post and western Cambridge's air raid siren was on Selwyn's tower.

Today, continental breakfast is served daily in hall but a full English breakfast is provided at exam time.

HOMERTON COLLEGE

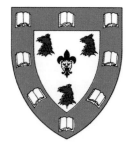

Homerton College is one of the best-known of Britain's teacher-training colleges. It prepares students for the Bachelor of Education degree. In 1844, the Congregational Board of Education was formed to implement the educational principles of the Congregational churches. It advertised for teachers 'between the ages of 20 and 30 - of undoubted piety – good health - decision and perseverance combined with humility - amiable temper - able to read and write well and apt both to learn and to teach.' In 1852, the board acquired a theological college in Homerton, a village in Middlesex, for the education and training of

7 a.m., there were daily walks in the open air and candles were snuffed out at 10.30 p.m. It was a progressive college and unique at that time because it admitted both men and women. (Women teachers were allowed to reach a lower pass level in mathematics because much of their time was taken up with needlework.) Teachers learned to encourage their pupils' interest in nature. Fees in 1870 were £15 a year.

By 1880 Homerton College was surrounded by factories and slums so the students' health was suffering. Meanwhile, Cavendish College had been founded in Cambridge on 10 acres (4 ha) of land 2 miles (3.2 km) south of the city to provide a university

education for the sons of professional men and farmers; it was hoped the distance from Cambridge would keep them in touch with their rural origins. The experiment failed through lack of funds, and in 1894

Homerton College left east London and moved into the empty, red Suffolk brick buildings of Cavendish College. There were one hundred rooms for women and thirty-eight for men, separated by the hall. Three years later the college gave in to pressure from the Department of Education and stopped admitting men.

Additional land was bought at the turn of the century, and lecture rooms, a sanitorium and art and craft studios were built. In 1909 Homerton became a non-denominational college for the training of teachers. Rules were still strict. On rising at 6.45 a.m. students made their beds and dusted their rooms. Silence was observed for most of the day. Assembling in informal groups was forbidden, and students had to pass each other on the right in the corridors.

In 1954 Homerton was granted a coat of arms. Queen's Wing was opened by the Queen Mother in 1957, and in 1977 Homerton became an Approved Society in the university. New science and biology laboratories and a new dining-hall were added in the 1960s and 70s, and in 1978 men were once again admitted to the college.

their teachers, supported by contributions from Congregationalists.

Life at the college was hard. The bell rang at 6 a.m. 'but any teacher may rise earlier if so disposed'. Classes started at

MURRAY EDWARDS COLLEGE

After the Second World War, there was a desperate shortage of university places for women. In 1947 a Grace approving the admission of women as members of the university was passed, and several women MAs felt it was time to provide more girls with the opportunity of a university education. So, in 1952, the Association to Promote a Third Foundation for Women in Cambridge was formed to investigate the possibility of founding a new college. The name New Hall was chosen by the association members.

In 1954, after fourteen months of hard fund-raising, the association had £25,000 in cash, promises and covenants that would provide an annual income of £1,500 for seven years. The new college became possible and the Association of New Hall was founded, members of the association being liable to pay up to £5 each if New Hall, as a limited liability company, went bankrupt. In 1954 the college opened with sixteen undergraduates and two senior members in The Hermitage, now part of Darwin College.

In 1960, after receiving a donation of £100,000 from the Wolfson Foundation, the college started to plan new buildings on a site half a mile (0.8 km) north of the city centre. Building work on a purpose-built college designed to meet the requirements of present-day students started in 1962. The Elizabeth Nuffield Foundation gave £120,000 towards graduate residential accommodation.

Women from New Hall and Newnham College began to row

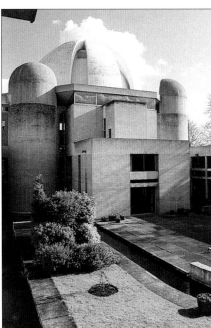

in 'The Bumps', the intercollege rowing races which try to 'bump' the boat in front on the narrow river, replacing it in the next day's race. They rowed on equal terms with the men and were quickly relegated to the bottom of the division, but in 1963 the Cambridge University Women's Boat Club won the first women's boat race against Oxford.

In 1964 Miss (later Dame) Rosemary Murray was appointed the first President of New Hall and some students moved to the new site which was opened in 1965 by Queen Elizabeth the Queen Mother. Later that year New Hall became an Approved Foundation of the university.

In 2008 the college received a generous donation of £30 million from alumna Ros Smith and her husband Steve Edwards. The college was renamed Murray Edwards College in honour of its first president and its benefactors.

The college was founded in a new, open way making more places accessible to women from ordinary backgrounds. It is committed to finding outstanding students from any background and supporting them, financially if necessary, throughout their education. It provides a supportive environment for the transition into the tough intellectual environment at Cambridge. This donation puts the college on a firm financial footing, allowing it to develop its many ideas for building on its fundamental values.

The college is laid out in a garden setting with Orchard Court, famous for its squirrels, and Fountain Court, famous for its goldfish. The library houses a large selection of feminist literature. The dining-hall is a short-armed cross surmounted by an impressive white dome reached by corner spiral staircases.

It is still a college for women only.

CHURCHILL COLLEGE

In 1955 Sir Winston Churchill (1874-1965) was inspired by a visit to the Massachusetts Institute of Technology to found an institution in Britain to train scientists and to encourage

first turf. Five million pounds was raised by 1966, and architect Richard Sheppard was chosen for Cambridge's first major work of modern architecture. The design incorporated nine connecting courts of three-storey brick and concrete buildings. A tenth courtyard was finished in 1968. Timber for the interiors was given by Commonwealth

seventy per cent of the students to study natural sciences, mathematics or engineering and one-third of them were to be post-graduates. The first Master was Sir John Cockroft, the nuclear physicist, the second, Sir William Hawthorne, pioneer of the jet engine. The college colours, chocolate and pink, were Sir Winston's racing-colours. In 1972 Churchill became the first Cambridge male college to admit women.

A chapel was built in 1967 after much controversy, some arguing the unsuitability of a chapel in a pre-dominantly scientific establishment. The library contains a Jean Lucrat tapestry presented by President Charles de Gaulle.

universities and industry to work together. From this idea, Churchill College developed. It was to be a national and Com-monwealth memorial and a living symbol of the 'gratitude of the English-speaking peoples' to the man who did so much to save Western values and freedoms.

An appeal was launched in 1958, and Sir Winston planted an oak and a mulberry-tree on the college site. In 1959 he cut the

countries. Some critics joked that the buildings looked like Sir Winston's discarded cigar boxes. The college sits in 40 acres (16 ha) of grounds, which contain sculptures by Henry Moore and Barbara Hepworth. and it is dominated by the hall's 50-foot-(15.2-m) high, triple barrel-vaulted, copper-clad roof.

The college received its charter in 1960 and full collegiate status in 1966. Sir Winston wanted

The Churchill Archives Centre, which was founded by past American ambassadors to Britain, opened in 1973 and houses Sir Winston's papers - from childhood letters to his last writings. It also contains papers of other famous people of the Churchillian era, and Lady Thatcher's papers are amongst the latest acquisitions. In 1992 the Moller Centre for Continuing Education was opened in the college grounds.

FITZWILLIAM COLLEGE

In 1869 the statutes of the University of Cambridge were altered to allow male students to become members of the university without being members of a college. They kept terms by living in Cambridge in duly licensed lodgings and were entitled to use the university libraries, laboratories and museums and to attend the lectures. They were able to compete for scholarships, to sit examinations and to be admitted to degrees. These students were under the supervision of a censor, whose office was in a house in Trumpington Street, opposite the Fitzwilliam Museum.

The house was reconditioned in 1892 and became the headquarters of the non-collegiate students. In 1874 it was named Fitzwilliam Hall because of its proximity to the museum. The hall became a residence for students who could not afford membership of an established college. In 1922 Fitzwilliam Hall became Fitzwilliam House. During the Second World War the house was disbanded, but it reopened in 1946 with over 400 men, making it at that time the fifth-largest student establishment in the university.

Fitzwilliam decided it should try to achieve collegiate status, and to that end funds were accumulated until the 1960s when it was able to expand. A new 7½-acre (3-ha) site had been

acquired about a mile (0.8 km), north of the city centre on land which had previously belonged to the Darwin family. Architect Sir Denys Lasdun designed the first buildings, a central block containing the kitchen, hall, combination rooms and library as a focal point, around which a community could evolve. The residential ranges were to grow outwards in a snail's-shell pattern as funds grew.

The first of the new buildings was opened in 1963, and in 1966, three years before its centenary, Fitzwilliam House was granted a charter by the Queen in Council and Fitzwilliam College was born. In 1978 Fitzwilliam admitted women.

The first residential blocks were built in dark brown engineering-bricks with exposed concrete floor slabs, flat roofs and regimented rows of floor-to-ceiling slit windows. The hall stands out as the most striking building in the college. It is topped by a large concrete and glass lantern with an undulating roof-line, which is particularly impressive at night when the clerestory windows shine out above the college with the opulent shimmer of a Middle Eastern palace. The New Court, a strikingly modern building designed by Richard MacCormac, was officially opened in 1986.

The buildings of Fitzwilliam College have been described by the author of a book on Cambridge architecture as 'a riot of sculptural invention'.

ROBINSON COLLEGE

Robinson, the last of the collegiate foundations in Cambridge, was founded by one benefactor, Mr (later Sir) David Robinson with a gift of £17 million, one of the largest single gifts ever accepted by the university. In 1981, on the day of the official opening by The Queen, Mr Robinson gave his college another £1 million. Born in Cambridge in 1904, David Robinson went to a local school and worked in his father's bicycle shop. In 1930 he took over a garage in Bedford and soon had a highly profitable business. He was one of the first people to move into retail television with his own firm, Robinson Rentals. He became a wealthy man and a successful racehorse owner noted for his generosity to worthy causes, particularly the Royal National Lifeboat Institution. He gave Cambridge a new maternity hospital, named 'The Rosie' after his mother.

Robinson is the only Cambridge college to have been founded for graduates and undergraduates of both sexes. It is also designed for use as a conference centre during vacations.

The college stands on a beautifully wooded 1½-acre (5-ha) site bought from St John's College. Bin Brook, which once supplied the monks' fishponds at the Hospital of St John, flows through the gardens and is represented by wavy lines on the college coat of arms. Building began in 1977. Architects Gillespie, Kidd and Coia of Glasgow designed a double ribbon of buildings with a fortress-like front and a drawbridge effect up to the main entrance and gatehouse. The castle theme is repeated in the portcullis-like trellis which breaks up the roadside facade. The college is a concrete structure covered by a skin of one and a quarter million handmade Dorset bricks.

The library and chapel are particularly impressive. The library, on three floors, has beautiful woodwork which won the Guild of Carpenters' Award for the contractor in 1981. The chapel is ecumenical, and members of all denominations participate in chapel activities. The interior is faced with Swanage multicoloured bricks, and there are two stained glass windows designed by John Piper. The larger, abstract one is particularly beautiful late on a sunny afternoon in summer. The organ, by Frobenius of Denmark, is one of only three by him in the United Kingdom.

The hall panelling, floor and furnishings are made of oak. The remainder of the college woodwork is Douglas fir. The first graduates were admitted to Robinson College in 1977. The first full entry of undergraduates was in 1980. Their accommodation is exceptionally comfortable, most sets having their own private bathrooms.

OTHER COLLEGES

RIDLEY HALL

Ridley Hall, opened in 1881, is a theological college which admits graduates of any university who have studied any subject and intend to take holy orders in the Church of England. Its foundation is closely associated with that of Wycliffe College in Oxford. It is named after Nicholas Ridley, a leader of the English Reformation, who studied at Pembroke College, Cambridge. He was appointed Bishop of London and in 1548 he participated in the compilation of The Book of Common Prayer. Ridley was excommunicated in the reign of Mary Tudor. At his second trial for heresy in 1555 he was convicted and burned at the stake in Oxford. Ridley Hall is a member of the Cambridge Federation of Theological Colleges which work closely together in theological and pastoral studies, worship and community life. It offers men and women a training suitable to their particular needs, both academic and practical. The original buildings were designed by C.S. Luck, and the chapel was built by W. Wallace in 1891. The fine reredos in the chapel was designed in 1949 by Sir Albert Richardson.

WESTCOTT HOUSE

Brooke Foss Westcott, Regius Professor of Divinity in Cambridge and later Bishop of Durham, founded Westcott House in 1881 as the non-residential 'Cambridge Clergy Training School' to provide a centre for the pastoral, devotional and theological training of Cambridge graduates who were preparing to take holy orders. In 1889 the first building was dedicated, and over the years the college became residential and was opened to members of other universities. Its constitution ensures that it has never become linked with any ecclesiastical party. It was incorporated by royal charter in 1960. In 1972 it became part of the Cambridge Federation of Theological Colleges, and in 1981 Westcott House accepted women to train for diaconal and accredited lay ministries. Dr Robert Runcie, former Archbishop of Canterbury, is a former Vice-Principal of Westcott House and so too is the former Archbishop of York, John Habgood. The lettering 'Westcott House' above the entrance was engraved by Eric Gill, and the rabbit and pig bootscrapers either side of the doorway were designed in memory of a former principal, B.K. Cunningham (coney and ham).

HUGHES HALL

Hughes Hall is the oldest, and one of the smallest, of the exclusively graduate colleges at Cambridge. It was established in 1885 as 'The Cambridge Training College for Women' but has admitted men and women equally since 1970. It joined the university as a constituent society in 1949, having taken the name Hughes from its first principal, Elizabeth Phillips Hughes, and is now an Approved Foundation of the university. The original college building is a handsome Victorian one erected by W.C. Fawcett in 1893. It is now listed as a building of historical importance. Hughes Hall is tucked away in a quiet backwater of the city with splendid views over the university cricket ground Fenners, the nursery of so many great English cricketers and the venue early each year of hard-fought matches between students and county players. Hughes Hall has maintained a historical connection with education, and about half its students read for the Postgraduate Certificate in Education, whilst others read for higher degrees or take advanced courses in a wide range of postgraduate subjects.

ST EDMUND'S COLLEGE

The 15th Duke of Norfolk founded the college in 1896 for the education of Roman Catholic clergy and laity from St Edmund's College in Ware, and it was known until 1986 as St Edmund's House. It was in 1895 that the ban on Roman Catholics attending university, which had been imposed by the state and the Church of England, was lifted, and the following year, on 23 April, Father Edmond Nolan came to Cambridge from Ware with just one young student, Charles Goulden. The moved into the presbytery in Hills Ro – 'the House' of St Edmund's College but on 2 November 1896 Father Nol and three students transferred to the present site of the college on Mount Pleasant. That day is traditionally ke as the college foundation date. Originally rules were strict, with the students rising at 7 a.m. and being required to stay inside the grounds aft 5.30 p.m. In 1952 St Edmund's was opened to laymen, in 1965 it became one of Cambridge's new graduate colleges and in 1975 it attained permanent collegiate status as an Approved Foundation.

WESTMINSTER COLLEGE

Westminster College is affiliated to t Cambridge Federation of Theological Colleges. It is the property of the Unit Reformed Church and trains minister for that church. Founded in London i 1844, the college transferred to Cambridge, where the present buildings were completed in 1899. They were designed by Henry T. Har Westminster is probably the most architecturally interesting of all the Cambridge theological colleges. The chapel has some excellent modern glasswork designed by Douglas Strachan and the Senatus Room is on of the finest oak-panelled rooms in Cambridge, with an impressive dome plasterwork ceiling. The dining-room ceiling carries four different versions the burning bush, the symbol used by the Presbyterian Church of Ireland, t Church of Scotland, the French Reformed Church and the former Presbyterian Church of England. The symbol and the motto of Scottish Presbyterianism, *Nec tamen consumebatur* 'Nor however was it consumed', is on the wrought ironwor spanning the gateway. In 1967 Cheshunt College moved into the Westminster buildings, taking their large collection of seventeenth-centur books and thus making Westminster's library one of Cambridge's finest theological collections.